THE ENTREPRENEURS BIBLE

EXPOSING THE SECRETS OF THE 1%

TABLE OF CONTENTS

Work Part Time Earn Full Time

It is not the amount of hours that you put into a working day as much as the amount of work you put into the hours. Far better to plan your day so that you can maximize your resources, instead of jumping from one task to another and end up doing nothing efficiently.

You do not need a large sum of money to finance a business proposition. All you need is a good idea and the ability to put together a business plan that will convince investors that you can make money. When people are convinced that you can make money, you should have no problem getting people to invest in your proposition.

A rule you should abide by is not to keep on working for your money indefinitely. If you do this, you become a slave to money. Far better to let money work for you. By investing your money in a business proposition where your returns are guaranteed ,you free yourself.

Take arbitrage investment in sports betting. An arbitrage is simply the purchase of securities from one market for immediate resale to another market in order to profit from the discrepancy
There are arbitrage opportunities in numerous markets. The one concentrated on here is the sports

betting market worldwide.

With the correct software this market can be exploited, giving guaranteed profits. If you know what to look for in this type of situation you can exploit the situation to give you a guaranteed profit. Coupled to the software is a FREE booklet detailing in specific detail how to exploit this market.

If the instructions in the book are adhered to the user can look forward to a guaranteed profit. There are people operating at the moment making a full time living out of arbitrage investment. This book will show you everything you need to know, to produce a very profitable and regular income from a loophole that has been brought about by the Internet and the masses of bookmakers that have sprung up and continue to do so. .This loophole can never be regulated or closed down and as the Internet grows the number of opportunities this loophole will make available will multiply

.There are many reasons why bookmakers may offer wildly different odds on the same sporting event .For a start many bookmakers overstretch themselves when offering odds—they try and cover every possible market to get as many customers as possible. This is great news for us because in doing so they will sometimes offer odds on events that they have little or no expert knowledge in .For example a bookmaker in the USA may offer odds on English division football yet he knows very little about it.

Not much money is needed to get started in this business as you progress and people begin to see that you are making a profit 100% of the time you are going to attract people to you, who are going to try and find out your secret of making money.

This is the time to start an investment club ,in your own neighborhood first and let it get known. You should be making conservatively 200% monthly on the money invested with you. Give your investors a return of 10-15% monthly on their money and the rest is pure profit to you. You should by this time be operating a very profitable business on OPM (other people's money)

Believe The Hype Making Millions Online

How much money can you make online? Are there really online millionaires?

Of course there are, but is it reasonable to expect that you can be one of them. Don't let the hype surrounding the emergence of opportunities cause you to lose your common sense. Millionaires are made by effectively assessing the needs of a market and having a product or service that addresses those needs.

The internet can greatly expand your ways to sell products or services. Some people have been able to use this to make a great deal of money. Some companies that operate only on the net have made online millionaires of their founders.

Before the internet there were auctions, but no eBay. With thousands of items sold daily, each one making a profit for eBay, there is no doubt that the founders must be online millionaires.

Before the internet there were bookstores, but no Amazon.com. Amazon is now outdoing traditional bookstores. Don't you wish you were the founder of Amazon?

Online millionaires start with an idea and a belief in themselves. They find a way to set themselves apart from the rest. Like real world millionaires, they often have enough faith in their ideas that they risk their own money and even seek additional funding elsewhere. Once they get started, they make themselves big enough that the other competition does not threaten them.

Online millionaires start early in the game. For example, now that we have eBay, people often forget there are other auctions. The only real competition Amazon has is traditional bookstores that were always there.

If you want to be an online millionaire, think of a need that is still largely unfulfilled. After that, you will probably have to believe in your idea enough to take some financial risks. If it doesn't work, you lose your investment. If it does, you might join the ranks of online millionaires.

Branding Do You Know Who You Are

There is such a lot of talk going around about branding, but what exactly is your brand and how do you use it to help you reach more people and market your products or services?

Your brand is the core of your marketing, the central theme around your products and services.

Your brand is not your Logo or your Company Name, unless of course you are Microsoft or the Yellow Pages online directory.

For people to come and hire you, or buy from you in droves, your brand needs to be crystal clear, attractive, exciting and powerful. In fact, your brand needs to be powerful enough to rouse your customers into action, and at the same time it needs to actively express you, what you're about and your uniqueness.

Once you're sure of your brand you also gain a tangible and easy way of talking to people about what you do. It makes it so much easier to do your marketing when you have it clear in your mind what it is you're selling in the first place.

"Exposing the Secrets of the 1%"

When you're creating your brand you are creating a memorable marketing message that will inspire people to take action and choose you over your competitors.

Here are five useful tips to help you find your brand:

Your Brand Tip 1

Your brand is the core of what you do. What feelings or emotions does your business inspire in you and in your customers? Did you know that peoples' decision to buy is based on emotions, not facts?

Your Brand Tip 2

Think about how you present yourself, not just on your website but when people see you, talk to you on the phone, or read your email. Is your marketing consistently saying what you want it to? Are people getting confusing messages from you, or is it clear from the start what you do?

Your Brand Tip 3

Think like your potential customer, try to get inside their head and see your products or services from their point of view. How do they experience what you do, and how does it make them feel?

Your Brand Tip 4

What is it you do that makes you stand out from the

crowd? If you don't think you do, then you need to think of a way that you can, because your brand should be somehow different from everyone else's, it's not enough to be just the same as others but better.

Your Brand Tip 5

What are your best abilities, do you know your greatest strengths? Choose an unbiased person, who knows you well, to help you decide what your top attributes are; your brand should be based around your unique strengths and abilities.

Ultimately, creating a strong, memorable, compelling and meaningful brand is essential for successful marketing, and something you can do with a bit of thought, and may be a bit of help from your (unbiased) friends.

The Art of Fast Money Making

In the immortal words of the great Zig Ziglar, "Money isn't the most important thing in life, but it's reasonably close to oxygen on the "gotta have it" scale" I am going to, in this article, refine your understanding about money. One of my greatest insights and valuable observations is to accept that money is not all the same. There are different species of money, you can divide money into 3 groups. Fast money, hourly money and credit money. The first is not based or connected to time, the other two are completely based around time.

Immediately we can observe when looking at these three species of money that one is very desire-able and the other two are worse and much worse. One stands head and shoulders above the other two and is the key to wealth. The other two lead to a life of daily roil and the poor house respectively.

Credit money, money you borrow to buy certain pleasures in life is the worst kind of money. Not surprisingly it is very closely connected to "hourly money" because to get credit money you must prove that you have hourly money…. a job. Then you can have access to credit money.

The point of credit money is to exchange time for the interest you pay. In other words, you can buy that car today and pay for it later. For a compounded interest rate of 10% to 20% you buy tomorrow's savings today. For people that prefer "hourly money" this type of transaction can seem highly desire-able. You don't have to wait 5 years to save for that car because you can have it now. The problem with "credit money" is the same problem that one gets with "hourly money" but much worse. Not only are we selling our precious time for money, but now we are selling and committing tomorrow's time for money today.

Hourly Money is the most obvious way to make

money for people. Hourly labor for hourly money. 90% of the world's population gets their money this way. A very inefficient way to get your money but you get it for sure. Security of a pay check is the number one reason why people strive to get hourly money.

Before reading this article, you may have never even thought about the three species of money. You may have not even considered that there is another type of money but hourly money and credit money. But there is. Fast money is what the 10% wealthy people strive for. The financial owners of planet Earth, the 10% cream of financial circles create money they don't work for it.

Fast Money – The art of authentic creation The art of fast money can be boiled down to one specific and it's that it's not connected to time. In this strange world, $100,000 in 10 minutes is nothing unusual. A million dollars in an afternoon is typical. $30,000 in 2 days is nothing special. You may balk at these time frames and amounts but that is the point of this species of money. The TIME component is totally irrelevant.

So if hourly money and credit money are intrinsically centered around time…what is fast money centered around?

SOLUTIONS

Fast money is not made by mindless time counting.

"Exposing the Secrets of the 1%"

Fast money is made by delivering solutions. An example of this can be found in the old dentist's joke. A guy goes in to have a tooth removed and the dentist tells the fellow it will cost $1200 to remove. The fellow replies, well how long will it take? The dentist replies 2 minutes. The poor guy is incredulous; you mean to tell me that you want $1200 for 2 minutes' work? The dentist replies, well sir, if u want me to take an hour doing it I can do that too.

You see the old fellow needed a solution to his problem. The dentist had that solution and had the tools to achieve the solution in 2 minutes. The fellow wanted a solution to his problem and THAT is what he was paying for, not the time spent, as his dentist adeptly pointed out.

Fast money and the art of finding and getting fast money can be found by finding people with urgent and pressing problems.

To get involved in this amazing fast money world, you must seek out these types of people. Find these types situations and begin providing your own unique and authentic solutions to get paid fast.

If you want to find thousands of Million Dollar Corporations with problems that need your help right now.

Are You Ready to Start Your Own Business? These are the 4 Key Questions You Must Ask.

Every year millions of people answer "Yes" to that question and every year that answer costs many of them money, time, confidence, and heartbreak. The Small Business Administration estimates there are 580,900 new small businesses opening each year and that number does not include the small one-person entrepreneurships that pop up every day. However even if you are your business's sole employee then there is still something to be learned from the SBA's numbers.

According to the SBA, two-thirds of new businesses survive at least two years and 44 percent survive at least four years. Two of the key factors in the businesses survival and ability to thrive: the owner's education level and the owner's reason for starting the firm in the first place.

How can you make sure that you are among the winners rather than the losers in this high stakes game? The answer is inside of you. You must ask yourself four key questions to determine whether your own small business will survive and thrive.

1. Are You Ready

Have you mentally prepared yourself for the switch from employee (or student or whatever label fits you currently) to boss. You are going to be the one making decisions now about everything from office products to product line. This total control is one of the driving forces behind many people who take the plunge into starting their own business but it is also one of the elements that drives new entrepreneurs crazy. When you start out there is an endless list of decisions that need to be made and new questions crop up every day.

Even more important you will need to remember that in a small business you will wear many hats. Even if you manage to start out with one or more employees you will each fulfill more than one role in your new business. And if you are running a one-man or one-woman show then you serve in every capacity from file clerk to maintenance crew to salesman to CEO. Can you handle switching from task to task and role to role like that? Are you willing to make those switches?

Similarly, have you prepared your family and friends for this switch in attitude. Your life is going to change

— probably pretty drastically — and that change can have a positive or negative impact on your family life and social interactions. It will make things much easier if your friends and family are supportive going into the process.

2. Where Is Your Niche?

Have you identified your niche yet? One of the reasons many businesses fail is that they fail to focus on a target audience. Yes, if you are a major discount chain then you can sell everything from peanuts to wallpaper but this type of business requires vast resources that just aren't available to the small business. But small businesses dominate the marketplace (creating more than 50 percent of the private gross domestic product last year) by finding a different approach — a niche.

Knowing your niche means you are better able to find, target, and maintain your customers as well as provide the best possible goods and services to that customer base. That focus is one of your best chances to not only survive but to thrive in a very competitive marketplace.

3. What Is Your Plan Of Action?

Another key factor in the survival and ultimate success of your business is how much planning you do before you open your electronic or physical doors.

You need to decide if your business will be based on the internet or include more traditional models. Are you going to work full-time or part-time at your new business? Are you going to hire help or go solo? Have you written (or at least outlined) your business plan? Dreaming, thinking and planning can save you much trouble and waste later when things are hectic and problems strike. Planning can also help keep you focused and to balance your spending and time.

4. Who Are You Going To Call?

At some point, no matter how experienced a business person you are, you will need help. You will need support, advice, tools, or information — or all of the above. One of the beautiful, and most frightening, aspects of growth is that it can lead you to places you never imagined. No matter how much planning and experience you bring to your new position as CEO the unexpected will arise. How will you cope with this? It is important to recognize that no business is an island. It is not failure to seek help. Failure is when your business shuts down because you didn't get the help you needed.

The best way to get timely help is to work on your support system while you work on building your business. That way you will already have a ready list of resources available that you can quickly tap into when emergencies strike. In today's world there are many marvelous resources available to you no matter what your business model may be. These include:

~ Publications (newsletters, magazines, books)

~ People (professional advisors, mentors, teachers, consultants)

~ Networks (organizations and forums in your niche as well as general business and marketing)

~ Education and training (tutorials, courses, and seminars)

After you have answered these four key questions you are now ready to ask yourself that one big question again — are you ready to start your own business?

Six Ways for Kids to Make Money

Most of us know the usual ways for kids to make money, which include lemonade stands, newspaper routes and mowing lawns. However, there are more unusual ways. Some of the ways listed below are from my own childhood, when I was always looking for another way to make money.

"Exposing the Secrets of the 1%"

1. Be a chef. At about eleven years old, I used to sell meals to my brothers (I had four of them). I got 25 cents for scrambled eggs or a sandwich, and more for more complicated meals. My brothers preferred to stay in front of the TV and let me cook for them. Since the food was already provided by my parents, the income was pure profit.

2. Computer whiz-kid service. Many young kids know a lot about computers. My nephew was getting paid for programming by the time he was fourteen, but even younger kids can show old folks how to use a computer and the internet for a fee. Learn a few more skills, and they can even set up computers for new owners who are using them for the first time. Letting grandparents spread the word would be a good marketing ploy.

3. Household carnival. I charged my brothers five cents for a wadded up piece of paper selected from a bucket full of them. Most had a penny or two inside them, but a few had a quarter. It was just one of my "carnival" events. I also had them throwing pennies at a bowl across the room, which I kept, of course. If a penny stayed in the bowl they won a dime. I'm almost embarrassed to say how much of their hard-earned paper route money I took from them.

4. Collect recyclables. We collected and returned cans and bottles for a deposit as kids. Now that more states

have return laws, it's an even better way to make a little cash. During the Cherry Festival, when I lived in Traverse City, Michigan, adults came to town just to collect the cans that people threw all over. With a 10 cent deposit, they were collecting more than $100 worth per day according to several of them. If the kids wear gloves, leave broken cans and bottles alone, and use hand sanitizer, this is a safe way to make money.

5. Personal services menu. If there are many people in the family, a great way for kids to make money is to sell their services. They can make a menu of things they'll do and how much they charge for each. It might include washing windows for 50 cents each, for example, and maybe $1.50 to walk a dog. If the list is copied, it could be handed out to all relatives and possibly neighbors too.

6. Yard sales and flea markets. If parents agree, kids can have Yard sales, selling not just household things, but arts and crafts and refreshments too. Parents might even take their kids to a flea market to set up a stand. I sold (as an adult) more than $1,000 of hand-made walking sticks one summer, while my wife sold hundreds of dollars' worth in pewter figurines glued to rocks, sea shells and crystals. Cookies and drinks sell well too. It's a great way to learn about business, and a good way for kids to make money.

Successful Entrepreneurs

Studies have shown that successful entrepreneurs possess these characteristics:

1. Self-confidence

This is that magical power of having confidence in oneself and in one's powers and abilities.

2. Achievement Oriented

Results are gained by focused and sustained effort. They concentrate on achieving a specific goal, not just accomplishing a string of unrelated tasks.

3. Risk Taker

They realize that there is a chance of loss inherent in achieving their goals, yet they have the confidence necessary to take calculated risks to achieve their goals.

Entrepreneurs are people who will make decisions, take action, and think that they can control their own destinies. They are often motivated by a spirit of independence which leads them to believe that their success depends on raw effort and hard work, not luck.

So which of these three main characteristics is the most important? Believe it or not, it has to be self-confidence. Without self-confidence, nothing else is possible. If you don't believe in your abilities, then the first challenge that arises may knock you off the path to achieving your goals. Here are a few things to keep in mind for maintaining a higher level of self-confidence.

Positive Thinking

Well, it all starts with a positive attitude, doesn't it? Believing that something good will happen is the first step. Negative thinking simply is not allowed. You must truly believe that there are no circumstances strong enough to deter you from reaching your goals. Remember too, that positive thinking can be contagious. When positive thinking spreads, it can open doors to new ideas, customers, friends, etc.

Persistent Action

Now all of the positive thinking and believing in the world is useless if it is not applied towards a goal. You have to take action; no excuses are allowed. This action must also be persistent. Trying once and then giving up is not going to be enough. Keep at it one step at a time. If you can't get by a certain step, then find a creative way to try again or just go around it.

At the beginning of this article we identified a few traits that are common among successful entrepreneurs. You should be able to look ahead and see yourself where you want to be. Now just maintain a strong belief in yourself and your skills, stick with it, and don't give up. If you can do that, you're already half way there!

Colleges that offer free & low cost tuition

An education is priceless. A college education is priceless and can be very expensive but how many people know there are 10 Colleges and Universities with low or full paid Tuition?

1. Berea College

Every student who attends Kentucky's Berea College receives a full-tuition scholarship worth more than $25,000.

2. Alice Lloyd College

U.S. News and World Report ranks Alice Lloyd College among the best U.S. colleges for graduating with the least amount of debt. This Kentucky school offers guaranteed tuition to any student in the college's 108-county Central Appalachian service area.

3. Webb Institute

The Princeton Review ranks Webb Institute among the Best Value Colleges in America. The school is known for providing a top-notch engineering education along with full-tuition scholarships to anyone who attends.

4. College of the Ozarks

Located in Missouri, the College of the Ozarks is a conservative Christian school that cheerfully discourages student debt. The school has been nicknamed 'Hard work U' because students work 15 hours each week to graduate tuition-free.

5. Curtis Institute of Music

The Curtis Institute of Music offers full-tuition scholarships to everyone who gains admission.

6. CUNY TEACHER ACADEMY

The City University of New York offers full-tuition scholarships to students who enrol in their Teacher Academy.

7 and 8. State of Washington Universities

University of Washington

Washington State University

Both the University of Washington and Washington State University offer need-based programs that pay full-tuition and fees.

9. Franklin W. Olin College of Engineering
At one point, the Franklin W. Olin College of Engineering offered a full-tuition scholarship to anyone who attends. The school has since reduced the scholarship policy by 50 percent.

10. DEEP SPRINGS COLLEGE

Located in Big Pine, California, this accredited two-year college offers full scholarships for each student, valued around $50,000.

Planning Ahead of Everyone Else to Win

What does it take to plan like a champion?

Well let's take a look into our minds a little bit to answer this question.

For these next questions, I need you to be extremely honest with yourself. No need to lie, no one else but you will know the answers.

1) Are you afraid to fail your plan?

2) Do you regularly plan ahead?

3) Does your plans involve EVERYTHING you ever wanted?

4) Do you plan ahead with your business and family in mind?

5) Do you visualize your plan being achieved?

6) ** How far ahead do you actually plan???

That wasn't so bad was it???

It's important to always ask yourself these questions. Doing so will ultimately lay out what it is that you want in life. Business & Family should always be considered together.

So let's take a look at why all these questions help you to determine what it is in life and how it will affect you forever…

1) Are you afraid to fail your plan?

Beating The Failure Blues:

Failure… Ooo no one wants to fail. Unfortunately for many of us, we tend think of failing when we write out our business plans. The reason we do this is because we've all failed at something before. Everything we do starts with a plan. Most daily plans are sub-consciously planned out before they are executed. This process only takes a fraction of a second. The ones we tend to remember are plans that we've "consciously" created. Most of these are ideas we've never finished, and projects that never even got a change to start.

They key to beating the "failure blues" is simply to train your mind to visualize everything you want from your plans. Viewing something you want should always resemble a movie clip full with: sensory rich images, along with sounds, smells, and sense of touch. This combination is what make visualization a success. This is true because our minds think in images. Visualizing your plans consciously will better help your sub-conscious mind to remember what it is that you want to accomplish. This also tells your sub-conscious mind you serious about this one.

1) Do you regularly plan ahead?

Come-on, be honest, do you actually sit there and make a good attempt to plan out your future, every single day? NO? Why not? Is it not that important to you?

Failing to plan is the same as planning to fail!

Planning everyday may seem like a lot of work to do but in actual reality, once it becomes a habit, it becomes second nature.

Study shows that it takes an average of 21 times for something to become a habit. For example, once you've driven your car 21 times +/- it becomes 2nd nature to you. Your sub-conscious mind takes over and drives for you

Your "conscious mind" is the captain of your ship (the brain). If you don't consciously make a direct command to your "sub-conscious" (the crew), nothing will ever get done. You must be strict with the crew for 21 days to make sure they will do their duties on a daily basis. After time, the crew will automatically know their own task by heart and carry them out for you.

Planning out every day will better define to your "Crew" what it is they are required to accomplish. It builds unity within your mind. This unity will ultimately be the staging point to reaching your goals.

2) Does your plans involve everything you wanted?

When I say everything, I mean everything. I have this little special note pad that stays on my desk at all times. Within it are countless ideas of everything I ever wanted at that very moment.

At that very moment meaning, whatever it was that I wanted to have in my life "at that moment" that would make me happier. Doesn't matter what it is. For you, exactly what right now would make you happy? A nicer car? $5,000 in your bank account? More clients? Better search engine ranks?

Writing exactly what it is that you want will give your mind a "TO DO LIST". Once your mind has its "TO DO LIST", your sub-conscious will search through your memory banks for an example of how to accomplish your "to do list". If your mind doesn't find anything within your memory banks, it will eventually start shooting out ideas and tips for your conscious mind to complete.

I should also note that writing down something is like etching it right into stone when it comes to your mind. It's like your mind is the piece of paper, you need to write something down in order for it to come back later and revise what it is that you wrote down.
3) Do you plan ahead for your business and family? Well why wouldn't you? When I think about my business, I think of what it will do for me, my friends,

and my family in the future. At the moment, I am currently not married nor do I have any children but that doesn't mean that I am not thinking about the future with a family in it.

Always consider business & family the same. They are a both part of yours and the their future.

4) Do you visualize your plan being achieved?

Visualization is the fruit of success.

Do you ever find yourself visualizing yourself in that car you always wanted? Who visualizes you and your family on some beach in Mexico somewhere? Who visualizes you winning the "entrepreneur of the year award"? ....YOU DO!

In order to be happier and more successful, you need to get better, you need to get better. I repeat, you need to get better.

Visualization should be a daily event. Take a moment every day, even for 30 seconds and visualize all the sights, sounds, smells, and feelings of everything involved with your daily plans.

For example, let's pretend that you have a presentation to do and like most people who have done a presentation, you are extremely nervous. Take a moment about an hour before the presentation. Visualize yourself walking into the meeting feeling great, confident, and relaxed. Hear the people having a good time, see them smiling and paying attention to you. Try to smell a nice cologne within the room that makes you smile when taken in. Last but not least, see all the people around you congratulating you on a job well done after the presentation. See yourself having a nice, warm, rich tasting coffee while discussing your successful presentation with your boss, employees or even your potential clients.

I guarantee you that if you make it a habit to prepare yourself with visualization in that fashion before any presentation, you will have better, more vibrant feelings afterwards.

This very same technique applies for your goals. You must see yourself driving that car, the way the air feels in your hair, maybe the way the engine sounds. Whatever you can think of that will let your mind wander into your goals and dreams, use it!

5) ** How far ahead do you actually plan???

This is by far the most important. The most important only because it takes a little from all the above questions I've talked about.

What is the furthest you've ever planned ahead? I'll put money on the fact that it's not far enough. Dare to be bold, be strong in your convictions. Don't be afraid to think outside the box.
So how far do I allow myself to plan ahead??? 200 Years!

No joke, my goals have included a timeline of around 231 years ahead in the future. See I don't only think about how I want to improve my life; I concentrate on something higher than life. I concentrate on my family history that is yet to be written. We all would like to leave a family dynasty to our future family members. Well, why aren't you planning ahead for it???

Don't be shy, afraid, uncertain or embarrassed, just do it. Keep doing it within your note pad that you write in. Keep thinking about your children, their children, your great, great, great grandchildren to be.

Think about them. Wouldn't it be nice if they could look back and say wow, my great, great, great grandfather had the vision, the dedication and the will to think of me? Think of the impact you could have on those to be. Even go as far as writing a letter to the individuals who will be in your family's future. Tell them what you have planned and why.

What if what you do now, affects someone 4 generations down the line in such a positive way that they feel the need to pick up where you left off? If it wasn't for your vision, it would of never happened. Better yet, it hasn't happened yet, so how about you pick up that pen and start your future right now, this very moment.

On that note, I won't keep you from writing your future.

Good luck & remember to see everything happen the way you want it to happen!

Business Plan for Online Business

Success online depends on having a plan, or more specifically a business plan. Often, very often actually, clients contact a designer with a burning passion to have a new web site online, and fast. Success takes more than waking up bug-eyed at 2:00am with the brainstorm of the century. You need to outline (and fill in) a real business plan and make adjustments before the official launch.

Citing an actual case for an online eBook business, I advised the aspiring entrepreneur to provide more information. Thinking through the questions and answers is a vital step towards developing a good business plan.

– Do you have a logo for your company?

– If no logo, what color scheme do you like?

– How many products (eBooks) will you offer?

– Are they all written and ready to go?
– Do you have cover art for your books?

– What system of e-commerce do you intend to use?

– Will you offer just pdf or exe formats, or both?

– Do you have the domain, plus registration and hosting?

– Do you have a projected launch date scheduled?

– How many affiliate products do you have to offer?

Defining what you do, your market, and how you intend to be different are vital considerations. You only get one chance to make a good first impression.

For an eBook online business, the competition is fierce and filled with some shady characters. When you begin the process of planning before jumping in, consider your image first and then answer "How will I establish credibility up front?". Weave this into your business plan and you should do well. Don't act before thinking or you may be perceived as just another online marketer.

To summarize:

1. Your Image – Have a stunning set of graphics for your corporate image to make a favorable first impression. Hire a pro if it's in your budget.

2. Establishing Credibility – solicit opinions from trusted people to give honest feedback about first impression and credibility, good or bad.

3. The Plan – Outlines or templates for creating a business plan are available free online. Get one. Use it. Be flexible, and change as you go.

In closing and from experience, I know that many startup online entrepreneurs neglect creating a business plan. Selling eBooks online without physical inventory except bits and bytes seems so easy. Your chance for success will improve with a real business plan.

Why Free Makes It Easy

Do you know what the most frequently used word is that people type in a search box on the internet? Knowing what this word is and using it to its fullest extent can literally EXPLODE your sales if you run an online business. Let me explain.

The all-important word is FREE!!!

The word that is used in searches on the internet more than any other is FREE. Everyone loves something for nothing. No one wants to pay for something if they can get it for free.

Think about all the times you have searched for something on the internet. Weather it was for information, a service, a product, in fact anything. Did you just type in the description, a keyword or phrase, or did you put 'free' before it? If you omitted the word free, when the search engines generated the results, I guarantee it gave you a list of 'related searches' containing the keywords you used with 'free' in front of them.

The benefit of giving something for free.

As an online business, if you offer a product, service or some information for free, it can have great returns.

First of all, it boosts your search engine rankings. As the word is typed into a search more than any other, having it optimized on your website will have amazing dividends.

Once a customer has found you in their search results, further use of the word free will draw them in even more. Giving them something for nothing if they visit your site is a big attraction. In fact it is such a huge attraction that I can't emphasize how important it is.

How giving something for free can make you money.

When someone visits your site to claim their freebie, several things can happen.

In order to get their free product, they have to give you their name and email address. This is the #1 reason for offering it to them in the first place.

It is highly unlikely that someone will buy something on their first visit to a website. And unless there is an excellent reason for them to return, they may never visit again.

By having their email address, you can contact them and remind them to revisit your site. You can offer them 'special offers' and affiliate sales through your correspondence emails.

It is a well-known fact that there needs to be an average of 7 contacts (sales pitches, remind revisits, offers etc.…)with a customer before they will actually buy something. The reasons for this are quite lengthy and are a whole other article, so let's stick to the matter at hand.

By being able to have the important contact with your customers, your chances of them making a purchase have increased significantly.

They learn to 'trust you', you become familiar to them and that is what often clinches the deal. You gain these things from your customers and then they buy.

So, that's how you make money from giving away something for free.

The quality of free.

The item that you offer, whether it be a subscription to an e-zine, an eBook, report or software, MUST be of good quality.
If the customer receives their freebie and the quality is poor, they will not come back to your website and

buy anything.

Even if you are the best website in your niche, offering the best deals, they will never find out, because they just won't come back.

On the other hand, if they are impressed by their free gift, they are more than likely to visit you website again and again. High quality, useful products are an essential if you want the 'freebie offer' to work for you.

How you can drive traffic to your website using 'free'.

Classified ads are a fantastic way to drive traffic to your website. The headline and description should be centered around the infamous "what's in it for me". That is offering them a freebie. This will entice them to click the link and visit your website.

You can post classifieds for free. Just type 'free classifieds' into the search box and choose from the 1000's of results that the search engines produce. Submit your ads often and the traffic will keep coming.

Other ways to drive traffic using 'free'.

Simply use it anywhere your ads appear. If you publish articles, reports or eBooks, put your offer in your resource box. If you use pay-per-click, use the offer as your ad copy. Advertising in e-zines, whether it's your own, an affiliates or bought advertising, again use the free offer in your resource box.

Choose carefully.

When deciding on what it is that you will give way, there is one piece of advice that is vital.

Make the free item appropriate to you audience. Whatever niche you operate it, stick with the theme.

If you offer an eBook on 'how to knit fancy tea cozies' and your business sells musical instruments, you will be heading for a problem.

The customer will visit your website to get their eBook. They will download it and probably be very pleased if it contained high quality information on 'how to knit fancy tea cozies'. When you contact them via email with for example a 'special offer on violin strings', unless by some highly unlikely, random chance that they play the violin, they will not visit your website again.

No matter how many emails you send them, their interest was tea cozies, not musical instruments. Why should they visit your site again? The fact is they won't.

So be mindful of what your own niche actually wants and give it to them. In conclusion, the more you offer freebies, the more money you will make.

It is one of the best traffic drivers and is a straight forward concept.

Now that you have this little golden nugget of valuable information, get to work. Plan what you could offer, to whom, when and where.

Decide on a product that you can legally give away. Make it something that is useful to your own niche market. Advertise it everywhere you can and your opt-in-list will grow very quickly. After all 'the money is in the list', but again, that's another article.

Below is a perfect example of the 'free' offer. I didn't make it up, it's for real and it works.

Every Entrepreneurs Worst Nightmare

Gone: Customers, sales, profits. Following is a simple little tale about how it happens.

"Jones was a typical entrepreneur who worked long hours and wore many hats.
"The problem was that all the hats screamed for attention. Jones solved the problem by wearing the hat that screamed the loudest.

"Unfortunately, this was only a temporary solution since all the hats kept screaming until they were worn.

"There was, however, one hat that never screamed. It never complained, whined or whimpered, even though it was lonely. It knew it was important, whether or not it was worn. That hat was right.

"One day the customers quit coming. The other hats became quiet; they no longer were needed. It was then that Jones noticed the hat named Marketing and how little it had been worn.

"'Why didn't I wear the Marketing hat?' thought Jones.

"For one thing, Marketing hadn't screamed for attention like the other hats. The other reason was that Jones was afraid the Marketing hat was too expensive to wear and would drain profits.

"But now there were no profits; the customers were gone.

"Jones put on the Marketing hat. It was time to get the old customers back, and to get new customers, too. It was time to wear the Marketing hat regularly.

"Even the other hats perked up."

Keys to Successful Online Entrepreneurship

Many people think operating an online business is good idea to make some extra money or to provide them with a way to work anywhere they want. An online business can be a very lucrative way to make money. A online business can provide you with more income and more freedom with your time.

The key to having a successful online business is to find one that you believe in and that suits your style. For instance, if you don't like selling things or contacting people face to face or by phone, then you probably need to choose an online business that does not require these things. If the online business is selling a product that you, yourself would not use, or don't believe in, then it makes it very difficult to make a believable presentation to others.

A online business is not going to run by itself, either. Most successful online business entrepreneurs would tell you that their online business got to be successful by working at it, putting in the time and the energy to make it a success. There is no online business that does not require some work. There are, however, some that do not require a large financial investment by you.

The best way to find the perfect online business for you is to do some research about the many different online businesses out there. This way, you can feel confident that you have chosen a online business that you will be good at and will generate the income you are hoping for.

Business Name How to Pick One from A Legal Perspective

A business name can be a huge factor in the ultimate success or failure of the entity. Unfortunately, many people fail to give a lot of thought to it prior to moving forward. There are many factors to consider including something memorable, a name related to your area of work and, potentially, the availability of the domain name.

Married?

Picking a business name is like getting married. You are going to have to stick with it till the bitter end. It is estimated a prospect will need to see your advertisement and business name at least 22 times prior to doing business with you. Once they associate your business with a certain name, making a change will be disastrous. Once you pick something, stick with it.

Naming Your Business

If you are going to be married to your business name, you need to make sure the bride isn't already married to another suitor. There are four significant issues to consider.

Initially, you must determine whether the name is already being used in your state. The Secretary of State controls the names of all corporations, LLCs and partnerships. Most also have a web site where you can conduct name searches. Even if you are a sole proprietor, you should check the name against those already registered in the state database. If the name is being used, you will need to consider an alternative.

Assuming the name passed must with the Secretary of State, you should check it against existing trademarks file with the Patent and Trademark Office. The "PTO" maintains an online database. As with the Secretary of State, you can conduct an online search to make sure no other business is using it.

In this day and age, many businesses incorporate a web site as part of their business model. If you are in this boat, you need to check to see if the business name is available as a domain. If it is, you should register it immediately. If not, you can either change your business name again or focus on a domain name incorporating your service or product instead of the business name.

Your business could be devastated if you do not take these precautionary steps. Imagine the negative impact on your business if the name has to be changed three years down the line. Take a breath before you select a business name. Like a spouse, it can be either a good or bad choice.

For Those Who Are Really Sick of Their Jobs Working for Others

Majority of people are trapped in the rat race having jobs working for others but do not know how to get out. This article offers a way out to achieve freedom through earning passive income. Internet business is recommended because it is exciting, rewarding and best home based business. Tips are given that are designed for professional business working from home.

If you're given a choice of making $500 as a one-time payment OR getting only $100 but paid this amount every month for 20 years if not for life, which would you choose?

If you work only once and get paid many times over, you're earning a RESIDUAL INCOME. Of course you'd choose the latter.
Elvis Presley today "continues" to earn residual income even after death because his records continue to "work" for him due to continued demand from his fans.

Therefore, it goes without saying that in order to build wealth, you need to tap into RESIDUAL INCOME.

Very often this is also referred to as "PASSIVE INCOME" because you could afford to be passive or non-active (i.e. not having to work) and still continue to receive income.

If you're like most people, you've been conditioned your whole life to think about income as a process of trading time and effort for money. Like the majority, you have been brought up to have only one major objective in life – JOB! Incidentally, if you don't already know, to many, JOB stands for "Just Over Broke".

You work hard in schools so that you could get good grades to advance to colleges and universities where you work even harder so that you could get a good and secured JOB. Once you've got the jobs you want, you continue to work very hard in order to maintain them and to climb the so-called organizational ladder of success.

As a result, many have fallen into the trap of the RAT RACE and you know very well you can't afford to stop because if you did, so would your income!
Although some of us could be drawing quite a handsome income, we're not truly "wealthy" because we're not free to do what we want and when we want with our money.

I've heard of many sad stories of "rich" EMPLOYEES not being able to spend badly needed valuable time with members of their families who're sick in hospitals because they could not afford to be away from their place of work for too long as their services are urgently required by their employers. Doctors could not even really relax and enjoy a long vacation for fear of the loss of income or patients while their clinics remain closed.

Can I really have PASSIVE INCOME? You might ask. Indeed, you can!

About 60 million people have access to the Internet – and yet it is still in its infancy. Every month millions of newcomers and thousands of businesses are reported to be setting up online. With this huge and expanding audience coupled with the fact that marketing and advertising can be done on the Internet so easily and at only a fraction of the costs of traditional methods, we now have a fantastic opportunity to be successful in online business.

Many companies have now aligned themselves with the Internet which has created many new paradigms in the past few years. Residual Incomes are made available to people from all walks of life. You can now make money online with simple and proven formula used by many to earn multiple streams of residual income.

However, don't believe what you've heard or seen in the Internet. Skepticism is encouraged because there are some dishonest people creating a lot of hype, unfulfilled promises and scams going around the Internet.

Fortunately, however, these are the exception, rather than the rule. You must be able to feel absolutely confident about using the services offered by "Internet Business Gurus" to help you make money online before you sign up. If you have any slightest doubt at all, drop it and move on to another.

Customers The Key to Successful Marketing

How well do you know your customers?

What is the primary reason your customers or clients come to you? Or purchase your product or service? What is the Number One problem you solve for them? Do you know? Are you certain? If you don't, your marketing could be missing the mark, and you could be missing out on sales.

Uncovering Your "Key Selling Point"

This is the Single Marketing Message that is the central message in all of your communications about your business, product or service. It can be difficult for small business owners to determine what their single marketing message should be. Why? Because they are too close to their business. And, because they are viewing their business from their side of the desk.

Keeping your marketing customer-focused can be a challenge

"Exposing the Secrets of the 1%"

Even if we know we should be looking at our business from our customers' perspective, it's often easier said than done. As a result, it is easy to get caught up in all the amazing features of our product or service and the reasons we THINK our clients are attracted or are buying.

But sometimes our vantage point is clouded by our own perceptions and beliefs. And those perceptions and beliefs may be inaccurate. So how do you pinpoint the real reason customers are attracted to your product or service and the true reasons they are choosing to buy?

There is an easy way to stay on track

Very simply, YOU ASK THEM! Okay, I know it seems obvious, but you'd be surprised how often we don't think of the obvious.

Your prospects and customers (and yes, even your rejecters

The Changing Pace of Advertising

Rapid advances in technology have changed everything from health care to communication. Now, as the latest technology becomes more accessible to a broader market, the advertising field is changing, too. Years ago, you could plan your advertising campaign around a few television commercials and print advertisements. And most companies would never have considered spending a sizeable portion of their advertising budget on the Internet. But in 2006, online ad expenditures are expected to reach over $16 billion.

Advertisers who want to reach their target audience and remain competitive in this high-tech world have to change with the times. You need to keep up with emerging technologies, what media types are most popular, and how consumers use what's available to them.

If you want to stay current and advertise your products and services in ways that reach your target audience on their turf, consider the following forms of emerging media.

1. Blogs

Blog is short for "web log," online journals that people without any HTML knowledge can create easily from any computer. They are frequently updated and usually include the owner's thoughts or musings on topics ranging from what's happening in the news to what they wear to work.

Companies or individuals can keep blogs. Company blogs usually promote products in what is known as an "adverblog." However, those blogs started by individuals without a commercial affiliation usually have more credibility.

About fifty million people keep blogs. And many different categories exist, including travel, health, and business. Blogs are popular because they provide a concise summary of news and information and give users power by providing information all in one place and on a timely basis. A blog dedicated to heart health, for example, will likely pull information from sources all over the Internet, so someone surfing for heart health information doesn't have to search several sites for the most up-to-date research about the topic; they can find everything they need on a heart health blog.

As far as advertising on blogs, ads are generally related to the blog topic. That heart health blog could be an excellent place to advertise a health food or exercise product. If you're interested in advertising on blogs, first look for help from marketing companies that measure hot blog topics and provide market research based on blog content.
2. Podcasts

Podcasts deliver digital audio and video files to a user via the Internet. The name comes from the iPod, but they aren't just for iPod users. A pod cast is an audio file in MP3 format that a consumer can download to their iPod, MP3 player, or computer. Then the person can listen to it over and over again, share it with friends, and save it on a computer's hard drive.

Six million people have downloaded podcasts, according to the Pew Internet and American Life Project. And of the twenty-two-million iPod owners, twenty-nine percent have downloaded podcasts.

Podcasts are an emerging media form that will continue to grow, and as this media outlet increases in popularity, the advertising possibilities will grow as well. Viacom, Disney, and Clear Channel all have radio-type podcasts, and even print media outlets use podcasts to broadcast interviews and other audio supplements to their print stories. For example, you can read an issue of a magazine and listen to an interview in its entirety on the magazine's website.

3. Gaming

Sixty-eight out of 108 million households currently play video and computer games, according to the "Digital Gaming in America" Ziff Davis report of August 2005. Advertisers can reach this market, which is mostly comprised of young males, in two ways.

First, advertisers can use gaming technology to insert their ads in popular games. For example, say you are playing a football video game on your XBOX 360. You'll see ads placed on the sidelines and on the scoreboard just like you would if you were in a real football stadium or watching a real game on television. Video games are also played online, allowing gamers to compete with opponents in other parts of the world. These games offer many opportunities to place logos and products that a huge audience will see.

Another way to advertise using games is literally to create your own game that the consumer can play online. This is commonly referred to as Advergaming. Many companies, such as Lipton and Mountain Dew, have used this advertising technique. The greatest benefit of these games is that they get people involved in the brand. Game designers create these games to interest a particular target audience, such as young children. Be aware, though, if you're marketing to kids, to closely monitor the game's content.

4. Mobile Advertising

Nearly 199 million people in the United States subscribe to mobile phone services. And every phone produced in the last year is capable of accessing the Internet. What does this mean for advertisers? It's another method for reaching the target audience. People now use mobile phones to search the Internet, play games, and instant message as well as to access sports scores, learn breaking news, and even check out horoscopes.

Mobile advertising presents a great means to reach the high school and college student markets with banner and video ads. Currently, mobile ads are simple and usually text banners. But down the road, as this technology continues to advance, cell phones may be capable of displaying television ads. However, this media outlet is not without limitations. Everything in your ad has to be cleared by the phone company, so you must consider the logistical aspects of placing mobile ads.

The High-Tech Future of Advertising

If you want to remain competitive in the future, technology will be key to your success. You should consider these four, and other new types, of digital media when putting together any advertising strategy, because traditional media outlets just aren't as effective as they once were. While it's difficult to predict exactly where the trends are headed, when you keep an eye on new technology, you and your service won't be left behind.

Angel Investor Groups

Angel investor groups are acquiring better acknowledgment as primary patrons in early-stage industry, attaining eminent rankings in industry-related annual surveys of private equity investment firms for entrepreneurs.

Angel assets are an up-and-coming part of the financial order, similar in significance to venture capital in the Seventies, according to experts in the field. Angel groups are starting to be viewed with importance by the present financial companies.

An important angel investor group is the Band of Angels, a formal assemblage of 100 current and former high-tech executives who put in their time and money into fresh, progressive startup companies. Band members have established reputed companies like Symantec, Logitech, and National Semiconductor.

Angels are characteristically high-net-worth persons or "cashed out" entrepreneurs who are involved in nurturing other entrepreneurs and are vigorously associated with the ventures they support, both pre-funding and post-funding. Recently, a growing number of angels have come together to develop angel groups, with a view toward putting together capital and investment proficiency. There are an estimated 200 such angel investor organizations in the United States.

Angel investor groups have emerged as important participants in offering equity capital to early-stage ventures. Angels have developed from investing as individuals and at times fashioning informal groups for particular investments, to forming official groups with vigorous venture-capital-like procedures.

With the venture capital society becoming more complicated, angel investor groups have also changed according to the needs of the new situation. A majority of present day angel investors are highly enlightened about investments, due to the presence of experienced angel groups who have common performances.

Any individual angel investor can obtain an immense advantage from the group's expertise if he decides to become a part of a considerate group of angel investors.

Nine Ways to Exit Your Company

As many of you may remember, singer Paul Simon said there are 50 ways to leave a lover. If you are a business owner thinking about how to leave your business, you have nine options to consider. Here's a brief summary of these options.

1. Sell or give your company to a family member;

2. Sell your business to one or more key employees;

3. Sell to your employees (ESOP);

4. Sell your business to other shareholders;

5. Sell to an outside third party;

6. Bring in an outside investor and keep a minority interest

7. Go public;

8. Hire a management team to take over and become a passive owner; or

9. Liquidate your business.

Determining exactly which option is right for you is a challenge that many business owners put off until it is too late. Opportunities pass with time. If you wish to "leave your business on your terms and on your time table," you need to be proactive about understanding your exit options.

We recommend that you follow a four-step process to determine which exit option is best for you. This process will ensure that your exit options are consistent with your personal goals and take into account the realities of your company and the marketplace.

Choosing a Path

Step One: Set Personal Goals. You need to identify your most important objectives; both in terms of financial goals ("How much money do I need from the exit to ensure my family's financial security?") and in terms of non-financial goals ("I want the company to stay in my family," or "I want to my key employees to be rewarded during the exit"). Establishing well defined and written objectives is the first step in the exit planning process. Doing so in advance of your exit gives you and your advisors the time necessary to make your goals a reality.

Step Two: Make Sure Goals are Consistent. With the help of your advisors you need to determine whether your goals are consistent with each other. Very often this is not the case. For example, many business owners want to receive all cash at closing when they exit their business. At the same time the owner may want to transfer the business to a family member or a key employee. Unfortunately, these two goals may be mutually exclusive. Family members and key employees often do not have sufficient capital to structure a transaction this way. A great deal of stress and heartache can be avoided by addressing these kind of issues early in the process.

Step Three: Understand Value and Salability Issues. Once you have defined a set of consistent objectives, you need to understand the market value and salability of your company. This analysis is important in that it will provide you with further direction and can eliminate certain exit options.

For example, if the value of your company is below what you feel you need to support a comfortable lifestyle after your exit, you may decide to take some time to enhance the value of your business or to do further financial planning to ensure you clearly understand your financial needs.

In addition to understanding the value of your company you also need to understand how salable your business is. Value and salability are not always the same. Salability determines how quickly a business will sell and how much leverage a business owner will have when negotiating with a buyer. Salability depends to a large extent on external market conditions. External conditions are things that are out of your direct control like business, market or financial conditions. For example, the option of selling your business for cash to an outside buyer may be eliminated because of a downturn in your business or industry.

We recommend that you work with an investment banking firm to determine the value and salability of your company. Only an investment bank that is actively talking with buyers can give you an accurate read of the marketplace and a "real world" sense of the value and salability of your company.

Step Four: Understand Tax and Legal Implications. The final step in determining the best exit path for you is to a path is to evaluate the tax and legal consequences of the exit options that are available to you. This evaluation will include factors such as legal structure of your business entity, how its ownership is structured, exiting legal agreements, as well as any changes that must be made. For example, if a transaction involves a sale of assets and the company is a "C" corporation, there would be significant adverse tax consequences. Good advice from your CPA and attorney can help minimize the taxes you would otherwise have to pay.

Using this four-step process, you will be able to narrow the list of exit routes to determine which one is best for you. The important thing is to start early.

How to Be a Creative Entrepreneur

There's a great line in Alice in Wonderland when the Queen says, "Sometimes I think of 6 impossible things before breakfast." I think you'll agree that this has to be creativity at its best! As a small business owner this is an ideal you really need to strive for ... but how on earth can you open up your mind to get to the point where ideas just spill out?

"Exposing the Secrets of the 1%"

Small business owners are expected to be creative and inventive, otherwise how could they run their own firm? If you have a sneaky feeling that creativity is not one of your strong points what can you do to stimulate your brain and get it kicked-started?

Be Unlimited

Too many people are 'limited thinkers'. They have their world placed squarely in a box and nothing can exist outside of that. If the newspaper reports something, then it must be right. If Joe next door says that something is impossible then he must be right. As a small business owner, you cannot afford to be a 'limited thinker'. You have to be an 'unlimited thinker'. Get into the habit of seeing no boundaries; decide that there are no taboos. Have the belief that with a bit of focus you can find a creative solution to all of your problems. This is the foundation for a creative thought process.

Be Future-Focused

Creative ideas invariably come when you 'look' into the future. The feeling of propelling yourself forward and seeing the problem solved is a great motivator. Do you think you could achieve the same result if you were backward focused? I don't think so! Train yourself to be future-focused, always looking ahead, not a traditional thinker who tries to find answers in today's world.

Be a Writer

Once you open your mind to the joys of creativity the ideas will quickly start flowing, as if someone has opened the flood gates! Just like flood water, unless you catch it the ideas are lost forever. Capture all your ideas by carrying a small pocket notebook with you. As soon as an idea pops into your mind, write it down. It doesn't matter how outlandish it is, you can look at it in the cold light of day later on.

The fact you are responding to the ideas by noting them will further encourage you to be even more creative – good deeds encourage more good deeds!

Be Clutter-Free

If you are naturally an untidy person, then get out of the habit! A cluttered office will lead to a cluttered mind. You cannot expect your brain to work efficiently when all it's doing is constantly reminding you how untidy your office is. To be creative remove all the clutter from your life and free your mind.

Be Action-Oriented

All of these points are great, but if you don't take any action with your ideas, then you may as well not have bothered. An idea is nothing but a thought unless you take a specific action to help bring it to life. Periodically review your notebook and see if there are any hidden gems, or ideas which can be quickly actioned. A lot of your ideas may not suit at all but in there somewhere is probably an idea, which if acted upon, could change you or your business. Commit fully to move forward on as many of your ideas as you can.

Don't be afraid to break down the boundary walls. As John Stuart Mill said, "That which seems the height of absurdity in one generation often becomes the height of wisdom in the next."

Let me close with one question – can you be creative enough to be dismissed as a dreamer? No? Then get practicing!

Entrepreneurs Find New Way to Finance Dream

Statistics show that more than one million people in the United States start a new business each year. That number would be much higher if all the would-be entrepreneurs had the financing required to get a business up and running. In order to accomplish their dream of business ownership, entrepreneurs are finding new and innovative ways to finance their new ventures.

According to Leonard Fischer, President/CEO of BeneTrends, one of these new financing options is the use of a person's existing retirement funds-a pension, profit sharing, 401(k), IRA-which allows that person to start the business he or she has always dreamed of without tax penalties, consequences or mountains of debt.

Under the Employment Retirement Income Security Act (ERISA), retirement funds can be transferred into usable capital for business investments or operations. If a person has more than $40,000 in a retirement account and is not currently employed by the company that holds those funds, he or she qualifies for this Small Business Administration (SBA)-recognized financing approach to start a business.

Retirement funds can be used for any business purpose, including:

• Purchasing a franchise or existing business

• Start-up expenses, such as purchasing property, equipment, etc.

• Working capital, including paying salaries, franchise fees, etc.

• Business expansion, such as funding additional franchises, locations, etc.

• Equity toward SBA or other loans.

The thought of dipping into one's retirement can cause some apprehension. Through this investment strategy an individual actually has more control over his/her retirement-instead of gaining minimal growth dependent on the stock market, those savings are actually being invested in one's own business. This approach often allows an individual to set aside more money for retirement than ever before.

"Today's entrepreneur faces an environment of tremendous competition, complexity and opportunity, so starting a business the right way is more important than ever," says Dr. Germain Boer, Director of Vanderbilt University's Center for Entrepreneurship. "This financing method is a good option for an individual who has accumulated funds in his/her retirement accounts."

The entire process generally takes two to four weeks to be completed, and can be done by phone, email, fax, FedEx and regular mail.

Working with an experienced employee benefits plan expert, starting a business is as simple as these four steps:

Step 1: Establish a C-corporation.

Step 2: The new corporation creates a retirement plan.

Step 3: Funds are rolled over into the corporation's new retirement plan.

Step 4: The new retirement plan purchases the stock of the corporation.

"So many people have watched their dream of owning their own business go out the window due to lack of funding options. We help people achieve that dream every day using money they already have," says Fischer.

If you're ready to explore this innovative financing option, be sure to consult an expert to guide you through the specialized process.

Online Business Work from Home Entrepreneur

Do you remember when you first heard of EBay. Online auction place. Who thought back then it would end up being so big and so many people would be using this auction site. Most of us are aware that you can auction off just about anything on EBay. People are making serious money selling products online at EBay. It is also a great resource to find those hard to find items.
Have you checked into the many possibilities on the web

to making some serious cash? There are so many ways to work from home and run your own business. You can buy products wholesale and setup your own internet store. If you do not want to stock items, you can find companies that will drop ship your products for you. There are even programs you can buy online that are a complete system that shows you how to do this. Did you ever think you could get your own business up and running for roughly under $100 dollars?

You can make money selling eBooks, writing articles for websites, creating websites...

There are so many ways to make money on the internet today. It just takes a little research and then time on your part to really learn the best ways to promote your idea and become knowledgeable about all the different ways to advertise online.

Do you have what it takes to become an aspiring entrepreneur to start and manage a home based Internet Business? Do you have the Entrepreneur Bug?

Seems with the growth of the World Wide Web more people are becoming entrepreneurs. Just what is an Entrepreneur? There are many definitions the simplest is a person who owns, operates, and takes the risk of starting a business venture. An entrepreneur can also be known as an inventor.

Do you need to invent a product to be an ruthless

entrepreneur? Absolutely not, just take an already existing product or idea and create a business and profit from it. Organize a business venture and assume the risks for it. Come up with your own niche to get clients, close deals and start making some serious money. Whatever you decide to get involved with you should make sure you really know your product inside and out. What are you waiting for? Start brainstorming today and make your dream of being independently wealthy a reality.

Superstar Growth Strategy

Here's a strategy that has catapulted even the smallest of companies into super-growth mode by learning how to find an army of top producers to grow your business.

No matter how small your company is, you can hire a sales force that can catapult company growth like you never imagined (one company that took this advice grew 500% in two years).

No matter how large you are, you're probably using the wrong criterion for hiring salespeople. How to attract star talent to your organization?

How to learn their weaknesses before you hire them (most companies have to hire a salesperson to find out all the problems they're going to have- this will show you how to get rid of the lightweights in just five minutes).

What about you? How would you stack up against top producers as a person who has a "natural" ability to build your business?

One-person armies who were struggling have learned to re-think their model to hire sales-staff, and suddenly they are sold-out.

Multi-billion dollar companies had to understand the unique psychological profile of top producers and why they should hire for psychological profile rather than background.

The type of person I'm talking about is someone you can put in a bad situation with poor tools, no training, bad resources and still, within a few months, they begin to outsell your best salespeople or build your company in ways you never dreamed possible.

Two things drive the superstar and they are both critical and work together perfectly when you can find them: empathy and self esteem

Step by Step Patents

Do you have an idea or an invention that you would like to get patented?? Are you confused or unsure of what to do to obtain an invention patent? The best place to go to get patent information is through the U.S. Patent Office. This patent information is available online at their website at uspto.gov. Here's a step by step guide to how the patent process unfolds.

The first step to filing your patent is to determine what kind of patent you need. There are 3 types of patents. The first is a utility patent. A utility patent protects how the new article is used and how it works. The next is a design patent. A design patent protects the way the new article looks. The third is a plant patent which is used to protect asexually reproducing plants that have been invented or discovered.

Once you have determined what kind of patent you need, you then start the application process.? The application must be filed with the U.S. Patent Office. The application describes the invention and it must state how to make use of the invention. It should also include why this invention should be protected by a patent. Documents, drawings, and testimonies should be included, along with the application fees.

The second step is when the patent examiner does a patent search to be sure your invention is truly new and not a copy of someone else's patent. The patent examiner will communicate with the inventor or the inventor's patent attorney if any questions arise. This part of the patent application process can take some time.

The third step is for the patent examiner to decide if the invention is truly unique and therefore in need of a patent. If your invention is unique, you receive a patent. If not, your claim will be rejected and you will have to argue against it.

You may go through a patent attorney or submit your patent application yourself. Patent attorneys can be found online or in your local telephone book. You may submit applications online electronically at the U.S. Patent Office's website at uspto.gov.

Once you have obtained your patent, it will be good for a number of years. Even so, it is possible for other inventors to try to copy your patented idea. Your patent protection is of no use if it isn't enforced.? To help ensure enforcement, you may wish to get the help of an Invention Development Organization (IDO). They will help you to keep your invention safe and to market your product.

How to Grow a Money Tree?

They say money doesn't grow on trees, but I think you can grow it on something even better! Your home computer. To make your money tree grow, you will need to give it a home and a place to grow. You can do this by creating your own website. Here are some basics steps to creating your own website:

1.Pick a domain name. Make sure the name relates well to the information on your website. If you can, make it short and easy to remember.

2.Create your web site using a web site creator, hand coding your own html, or a combination of both.

3. You will need to sign up for a hosting account to get your website online.

Next you will need to plant the money tree seed by developing your product so it can grow:

1.The fastest and easiest way to create a product to sell on your new web site is to create an information product (e-book, audio, etc.). It's very low cost or free to create, and everything is automatic and electronic. That means there is no overhead and no products to ship!

2.You may also want to consider borrowing some seeds while you make your own. You can do this but signing up with other companies that sell information products and selling their products for a commission. This is a great way to get started and test the markets to see what's selling. You also build relationships with companies and that very well could be a marketing advantage after you finish your product.

Finally you will need to nourish your tree by watering it with traffic.

There are three main way to get traffic to your website

1.You can buy traffic through sites like google. With this method you pay each time someone searches for your key words and they click on your link to your site. Through google you will be paying $.05 each click and up.

2.You can email you mailing list you made over time. Send out a promotional email and get your previous traffic coming back. Just be careful not send out too many, or they will become annoyed and turned off to all your other emails.

3.Partner up with your competition. You can get your competitors to send out your promotional emails by offering them a commission. Your competitors can become one of your best assets!

Maintain your tree by watering it with plenty of traffic, and give it plenty of love by updating your material!

Fallow these easy steps and your money tree should be ready for harvest in no time.

Women Entrepreneurs Prove Its Not Just a Man's World

I had the honor of speaking this week at a women's business association luncheon on the topic of entrepreneurship. When I mentioned to my wife the day before that I was speaking to group of women entrepreneurs she asked, "Why on earth would they ask you to speak?"

In her defense, my dear wife has no idea what I do for a living. She's never read a single one of the several hundred columns I've written. She's never attended a function where I'm speaking or sat in the audience at any of my seminars.

She just knows that we live a very comfortable lifestyle and believes me when I tell her our money doesn't come from the drug trade.

Beyond that, she's incredibly happy in her ignorance of her husband's skills.

When I feigned hurt feelings she waved a hand at me and said, "My point is, what in the world can a man tell a roomful of women that they don't already know?"

Henny Youngman, Ralph Cramden, Rodney Dangerfield, Tim Knox. At least I'm in good company.

But she had a point. What the heck did I know about women in business? So as not to look like a total idiot in front of this group of what I now call "womentrepreneurs" I decided to do a little research on the topic.

Here's what I discovered: while some still believe it's a man's world, when it comes to business, women are catching up fast.

According to the Center For Women's Business Research there are over 10 million women-owned businesses in the US, employing 18 million people and generating $2.32 trillion in sales.

Women start businesses at two times the rate of men and women-owned businesses account for 28 percent of all businesses in the United States and represent about 775,000 new startups per year and account for 55% of new startups.

One thing that I found particularly interesting was that the top growth industries for women-owned businesses in recent years were construction, wholesale trade, transportation/communications, agribusiness and manufacturing, industries traditionally dominated by men.

In the past 25 years the number of women-owned firms in the US has doubled, employment has increased four-fold and their revenues have risen five-fold.

Here is the question I sought particularly to answer: Do women approach business differently than men? I've been compared to a bull in a china shop when it comes to business. Would some female counterparts approach things differently? More gracefully, perhaps? As my lovely bride would say, "Duh."

In her book, How to Run Your Business Like a Girl, Elizabeth Cogswell Baskin explored common female traits and how women entrepreneurs – and perhaps men, as well – can use those traits to their entrepreneurial advantage.

Baskin reported that women tend to use three unique strengths more than their male counterparts: trusting their intuition, focusing on relationships, and putting more emphasis on keeping their life in balance.

Trust Your Gut

Women are much more likely to make a decision based on a gut feeling. Women may gather the facts and figures necessary to back up that feeling, but they generally know what they want to do based on intuition.

Build Strong Relationships

Men play the game of business like a sport. They are out to win and dominate. "Women," Baskin says, "are much more interested in establishing a connection."

Find A Balance Between Work and Life.

A number of women interviewed for this book cited on quality of life as their reason for starting a business, alluding to their desire to find a way to juggle family and work. "If having more time for your family is important to you, find a way to work that into your day. It's not so much how much work you do, but being able to decide when you'll do it."

Baskin offers one more piece of advice to women in the early stages of their business:

You Don't Have To Know Everything.

My wife would argue this point because she really does know everything, but Baskin says when it comes to business, thinking you know everything is not the key to success.

"It's amazing how many women say they didn't know anything when they started their business," Baskin said. "Don't be afraid to ask for help – you don't have to be perfect at everything."

Running A Business On Limited Resources

When I first started my business, I went to the bank for a business loan. Simple enough, right? I had my business plan in order, an itemized list of everything that I would need to successfully run my business, and all the necessary documents. To put it plainly, I was turned down. Why? Not because I did not have the credit to back it up, or did not have a good business plan. The reason the bank man gave me was "because I did not understand that over 90% of businesses fail within the first year, and that I was not prepared in case mine did."

While I understand he was attempting to look out for my best interest, I felt cheated. He was not even going to give me the opportunity to fail. On some level, everyone that goes into business for themselves understand that chances are, the business will not make it past its first year, and I was no different. The only thing was I had faith in myself that I would not give up trying. The loan processor took that as I would spend my life savings before giving up, and he did not want to see me financially ruin myself.

So what did I do? I set out on the adventure on my own, only using the limited resources and financial backing that I had. I bought second hand office supplies and furniture. I bought the small cheap laptop instead of the multi-thousand-dollar computer specifically designed for what I would be doing. Without the proper money for advertising, I had to get creative. My advertising methods was unconventional, but they worked. I found that I did not need large amounts of money in order to get my business to the world.

So would I have been so successful had the loan processor gave me the business loan I asked for? I am not sure, because after all, I made it without the money, what would have happened if I would have had the proper money for advertising? Whatever the case may have been, I am glad he did not, because I am not better able to understand the limited resources that many small businesses face.

So how can you run your business on limited resources? Here are a few things that I learned along the way.

1) New vs. Used- When starting your business, you do not need everything to be "new." Second hand items cost substantially less then new items, and work just as well. Plus, if you think about it, customers will be more comfortable around your office if it feels "broke-in", rather than new and sterile. It gives them the feeling that you have been in business awhile.

2) Creative Advertising- You do not need the hundreds of dollars that it takes to place ads in papers or put commercials on TV. It costs very little to design and print you own flyers and put them in places where your potential clients would gather. Turn your vehicle into a

moving billboard by investing in a vinyl signage for your doors or windows. The best thing? Face to Face meetings with your potential clients do not cost a penny, so look for every opportunity to talk with our potential clients.

3) Work At Home- Depending on your type of business, you may consider working at home rather than renting office space. This will save you a lot of money on rent and furnishing an office. Once your business becomes more successful, then you can always rent office space later.

Overall, be thankful for the struggles that you go through now, because in the future, they will have been well worth it. Plus, it will give you a better understanding when it comes to other small businesses.

And, no matter what, never give up on yourself.

Trapped On the Treadmill Work Life Balance

Workers suffering burnout are making mistakes. It's depressingly predictable: these mistakes cost money, compromise safety and may even put lives at risk. Work-life balance is a subject with broad points of view but Corporate America is finally responding to this demand. Actually it's been a matter of company survival. Corporations expecting employees to forego family time will not find the Ace Employee. Increased irritability means less production as more as more workers struggle to 'keep it all together'.

Smart companies are recognizing employee needs for work-life balance and are providing an environment that encourages that balance. Yet, limiting this to quick fixes like flexible working hours, or part time hours for working mothers is not dealing with the real reasons why people are feeling disillusioned with their working life. It has more to do with long hours, constant overtime, bullying bosses, and the continual cutbacks that keep many on a frayed tightrope.

The core problem lies inside the minds of management — obsessive drives, insane greed for money and power, ambition gone awry and a foolish disregard of anything void of short-term results. Even with limited changes, management still treats underlings like a herd of cows milking every ounce of effort possible. That's not about to change when it's driven by a 'winner takes all' ideology and contempt for those unable to keep up.

In a 2006 study, men were more likely to report depression, increased drinking and smoking, and suicidal thoughts. Women on the other hand were more likely to report anxiety, uncontrolled crying, migraines, sleeplessness and persistent petty ailments.

Patrick learned the hard way – at 40 he had risen to Senior Attorney for a small insurance company. His all-consuming job of 80-100 hours each week leaves his wife complaining that he was never home, and even when he is, he's useless. His children are in bed when he finally calls it a day, and often he sleeps in his clothes on top of the covers to get a head start the following morning at 5am.

Patrick admits he is spread too thin but if he doesn't run at breakneck speed, everything will overtake him – as if he's on a treadmill with no controls. He is gaining weight catching junk food on the run and drinking more to "unwind" as he puts it. But a long weekend with friends changed everything. Patrick was on the phone constantly and his wife felt more like she had joined their friends as a single. Vexed and defeated, she finally blurted out: "I'm done! I don't want to do this anymore".

Often a wakeup call follows a crisis. To save his marriage

and family Patrick had to adopt a family-first policy. He laid his decision on the corporate table – no more weekends, home for dinner every night, no phone calls after 7pm! The silence was deafening.

Determined, he turned to the Internet and a new road to entrepreneurship. The dream of perfect harmony in work and home has worked for many who have chosen this road. Enjoyable, stress free and rewarding, they learned to love the risk factor because, as entrepreneurs they were able to see a direct benefit from the fruits of their own labor.

Entrepreneurs have a rosy view of their work-life balance because they love their boss. It's a big change from putting in 100 hours a week to please management by putting job first and everything else second, third or not at all. The new pioneers of this millennium will not be charging into the workplace as soon as they graduate. They will take their time and enjoy the trip. Ah well, the world doesn't need any more lawyers.

Dare to Be Different

Adding value to your site, service, or product is one of the most over looked and under rated strategies for improving your internet business.

The internet and modern technology makes it possible for anyone to offer that little something extra that nobody else does, and usually at no additional cost.

Why: First, let's look at why this is a good business practice.

It's a good thing to do because you will make more money!

What: Now let's look at what value adding is!

Value adding is giving surprise high quality and useful gifts.

It's giving something that your competitors aren't offering.

It's promising the world and delivering the universe.

It's taking care of your clients and always providing something that your clients need and want, when and where they want it.

How: Now let's look at the different ways we can do this.

If you receive a free gift from someone when you don't expect it, do you remember that person?

Answer; yes usually.

How can we do this?

Look at the example below for an idea!

If you subscribe to a newsletter or e-zine, what do you expect?

You expect to get what you subscribed for, right?

Now imagine that you subscribed for a newsletter that distributes information about Poodle breading in France, and when you open the conformation email you find you've also received a free eBook containing 20 poodle grooming tips and Grandmas secret poodle pampering techniques. (a book that normally sells for $29)

Wouldn't that make you more likely to open and read the next issue and the next etc.?

That's one simple example, but where do you get the eBook from? You make it! If you are distributing a poodle breeding newsletter, you might know something about grooming, or know some people that could help you put together the necessary information. Then you can wrap that up in an eBook cover and then send it around to a variety of sites that will post it for you for free and you can sell on your own site, if you have one. (I can see that there are several more articles just on making e-books, posting them on other people's sites, and setting up a shop front.)

Back to the Poodles! So you can see that by offering this free gift you have achieved several things.

1. You have developed a product (at no cost to you) that you can sell and make a profit on.

2. You have used that product to increase the chances of your new subscriber opening your next email.

3. You have promoted you site/service to other internet marketers that you may wish to do a joint venture with at some time. (see my article on Joint ventures)

Another way to add value for less effort is to offer a 110 percent guarantee instead of a 100 percent.

Another is to make your 20 tips into 30 or more etc, get the idea? It's all just a matter of finding ways that you can give more.

The more you give the more you will receive.

Factoring Basics

Most sales to commercial clients usually carry 30 to 60-day payment terms. This means that as a supplier, you must deliver your products or services now. However, your client has between 30 to 60 days to pay you.

This creates a significant challenge for owners of small and midsize businesses. The problem is simple. Your clients want to pay you in 30 to 60 days, but you must pay rent, payroll and your suppliers now. As you can see, the math does not work. Unless you have a substantial bank account, this leads to an almost impossible situation.

If you are in this situation, it is also very likely that the bank will not be able to help you. As you well know, banks only lend to businesses that have three years of profitable operations and significant hard collateral. If you do not qualify for bank financing, your best bet may be to consider factoring.

Factoring is a business financing tool that helps business owners who cannot afford to wait 30 to 60 days to get paid by their commercial customers. Factoring provides you with the necessary funds to meet payroll, make rent and pay your suppliers on time.

As opposed to bank financing, factoring is easy to qualify for. The main requirements are that you have a profitable business with a strong roster of commercial clients. For the factoring company, your best collateral is the invoices from your strong customers.

Factoring is also easy to use. It enables you receive a substantial portion of your billings within a day of invoicing. It reduces the time you wait to get paid from 60 days to 2 days. The transaction is usually structured as a two installment sale of an invoice. The first installment, called the advance, is paid to you immediately. The advance can be anywhere between 70% and 90% of the gross value of the invoice. The remaining portion (10% – 30%) is held as a reserve to cover disputes and charge backs. The reserve is rebated as soon as the invoice is paid in full. The factoring company will charge a small fee for this service.

Factoring financing is an ideal tool for companies that are growing and that cannot afford to wait to get paid by the clients. It helps you to stabilize your financial situation and positions you for growth.

Do Not Get Above Your Business

Young men after they get through their business training, or apprenticeship, instead of pursuing their avocation and rising in their business, will often lie about doing nothing. They say; "I have learned my business, but I am not going to be a hireling; what is the object of learning my trade or profession, unless I establish myself?'"

"Have you capital to start with?"

"No, but I am going to have it."

"How are you going to get it?"

"I will tell you confidentially; I have a wealthy old aunt, and she will die pretty soon; but if she does not, I expect to find some rich old man who will lend me a few thousands to give me a start. If I only get the money to start with I will do well."

There is no greater mistake than when a young man believes he will succeed with borrowed money. Why? Because every man's experience coincides with that of Mr. Astor, who said, "it was more difficult for him to accumulate his first thousand dollars, than all the succeeding millions that made up his colossal fortune." Money is good for nothing unless you know the value of it by experience. Give a boy twenty thousand dollars and put him in business, and the chances are that he will lose every dollar of it before he is a year older. Like buying a ticket in the lottery; and drawing a prize, it is "easy come, easy go."

He does not know the value of it; nothing is worth anything, unless it costs effort. Without self-denial and economy; patience and perseverance, and commencing with capital which you have not earned, you are not sure to succeed in accumulating. Young men, instead of "waiting for dead men's shoes," should be up and doing, for there is no class of persons who are so unaccommodating in regard to dying as these rich old people, and it is fortunate for the expectant heirs that it is so.

Nine out of ten of the rich men of our country to-day, started out in life as poor boys, with determined wills, industry, perseverance, economy and good habits. They went on gradually, made their own money and saved it; and this is the best way to acquire a fortune. Stephen Girard started life as a poor cabin boy, and died worth nine million dollars. A.T.

Stewart was a poor Irish boy; and he paid taxes on a million and a half dollars of income, per year. John Jacob Astor was a poor farmer boy, and died worth twenty million. Cornelius Vanderbilt began life rowing a boat from Staten Island to New York; he presented our government with a steamship worth a million of dollars, and died worth fifty million.

"Exposing the Secrets of the 1%"

"There is no royal road to learning," says the proverb, and I may say it is equally true, "there is no royal road to wealth." But I think there is a royal road to both. The road to learning is a royal one; the road that enables the student to expand his intellect and add every day to his stock of knowledge, until, in the pleasant process of intellectual growth, he is able to solve the most profound problems, to count the stars, to analyze every atom of the globe, and to measure the firmament this is a regal highway, and it is the only road worth traveling.

So in regard to wealth. Go on in confidence, study the rules, and above all things, study human nature; for "the proper study of mankind is man," and you will find that while expanding the intellect and the muscles, your enlarged experience will enable you every day to accumulate more and more principal, which will increase itself by interest and otherwise, until you arrive at a state of independence. You will find, as a general thing, that the poor boys get rich and the rich boys get poor. For instance, a rich man at his decease, leaves a large estate to his family. His eldest sons, who have helped him earn his

fortune, known by experience the value of money; and they take their inheritance and add to it. The separate portions of the young children are placed at interest, and the little fellows are patted on the head, and told a dozen times a day, "you are rich; you will never have to work, you can always have whatever you wish, for you were born with a golden spoon in your mouth."

The young heir soon finds out what that means; he has the finest dresses and playthings; he is crammed with sugar candies and almost "killed with kindness," and he passes from school to school, petted and flattered. He becomes arrogant and self-conceited, abuses his teachers, and carries everything with a high hand. He knows nothing of the real value of money, having never earned any; but he knows all about the "golden spoon" business.

At college, he invites his poor fellow-students to his room, where he "wines and dines" them. He is cajoled and caressed, and called a glorious good follow, because he is so lavish of his money. He gives his game suppers, drives his fast horses, invites his chums to fetes and parties, determined to

have lots of "good times." He spends the night in frolics and debauchery, and leads off his companions with the familiar song, "we won't go home till morning." He gets them to join him in pulling down signs, taking gates from their hinges and throwing them into back yards and horse-ponds. If the police arrest them, he knocks them down, is taken to the lockup, and joyfully foots the bills.

"Ah! my boys," he cries, "what is the use of being rich, if you can't enjoy yourself?"
He might more truly say, "if you can't make a fool of yourself;" but he is "fast," hates slow things, and doesn't "see it." Young men loaded down with other people's

money are almost sure to lose all they inherit, and they acquire all sorts of bad habits which, in the majority of cases, ruin them in health, purse and character. In this country, one generation follows another, and the poor of to-day are rich in the next generation, or the third. Their experience leads them on, and they become rich, and they leave vast riches to their young children. These children, having been reared in luxury, are inexperienced and get poor; and after long experience another generation comes on and gathers up riches again in turn. And thus "history repeats itself," and happy is he who by listening to the experience of others avoids the rocks and shoals on which so many have been wrecked.

"In England, the business makes the man." If a man in that country is a mechanic or working-man, he is not recognized as a gentleman. On the occasion of my first appearance before Queen Victoria, the Duke of Wellington asked me what sphere in life General Tom Thumb's parents were in.

"His father is a carpenter," I replied.

"Oh! I had heard he was a gentleman," was the response of His Grace.

In this Republican country, the man makes the business. No matter whether he is a blacksmith, a shoemaker, a farmer, banker or lawyer, so long as his business is legitimate, he may be a gentleman. So any "legitimate" business is a double blessing it helps the man engaged in it, and also helps others. The Farmer supports his own family, but he also benefits the merchant or mechanic who needs the products of his farm. The tailor not only makes a living by his trade, but he also benefits the farmer, the clergyman and others who cannot make their own clothing. But all these classes often may be gentlemen.

The great ambition should be to excel all others engaged in the same occupation.

The college-student who was about graduating, said to an old lawyer:

"I have not yet decided which profession I will follow. Is your profession full?"

"The basement is much crowded, but there is plenty of room up-stairs," was the witty and truthful reply.

No profession, trade, or calling, is overcrowded in the upper story. Wherever you find the most honest and intelligent merchant or banker, or the best lawyer, the best doctor, the best clergyman, the best shoemaker, carpenter, or anything else, that man is most sought for, and has always enough to do. As a nation, Americans are too superficial– they are striving to get rich quickly, and do not generally do their business as substantially and thoroughly as they should, but whoever excels all others in his own line, if his habits are good and his integrity undoubted, cannot fail to secure abundant patronage, and the wealth that naturally follows. Let your motto then always be "Excelsior," for by living up to it there is no such word as fail.

The Entrepreneurial Edge

Some would say that big business has it made; I on the other hand believe that there will always be a special place for the little business guy. Entrepreneurs have an edge over their bigger competitors. So while the Amazon's of the world are struggling to break even from their multibillion-dollar overheads, the smaller Dot coms are already realizing profits. What advantages do the "little" guys have in the marketplace? Below is how to "think like a startup" and realize greater success.

HOW TO KEEP THE ENTREPRENEURIAL EDGE

1) STAY IN TOUCH WITH YOUR CUSTOMERS

Ever heard of the 80/20 rule? The old adage says that 80% of your business will come from 20% of your customers. In business, the customer is king. It's far easier to sell to an existing customer than to find a new one. So, once you get a customer, you need to service the heck out of them.

So how do you make your customers feel like they are number one? By letting them know that they are top priority. This means answering your own phone, replying quickly to email requests. It means staying in regular communication with your customers. Keep up a good rapport. Send an occasional email asking them what's new. Mail birthday cards or a customer anniversary card. Gestures like these can build close, long lasting customer relations and goes a long way to building customer loyalty.

In addition to building stronger customer relationships, keeping in touch with your customer base can enable dot coms to offer one to one marketing. By identifying your customers' needs and buying habits, you can personalize product packages and service offerings to meet your customer's individual needs.

2) LISTEN TO THE BEAT OF THE STREET

If small business owners want to keep their head above water, they need to closely monitor their environments. By "listening" to the pulse, you can think proactively rather than reactively. This means spotting things when they are coming so you can act quickly and take advantage.

Web stats – Do you look at your web stats regularly? Or are you guilty of being too "busy" to make time? Unless you regularly look at your web traffic reports, they probably will read like a foreign language to you. By looking at your web reports regularly, you'll be able to spot trends. What pages are your visitors going to? What is the hits-to-sales ratio? What can you do to improve that number?

Feedback – Another way to "listen to the beat" is to get feedback from your customers. Try to be on a first name basis with your customers. Ask them how they are doing and if there is anything you could assist them with. The answers you'll receive will be worth their weight in gold.

Industry news – Keep up with the industry by reading everything you can get your hands on. When you work in "living room central" it's easy to let yourself be isolated from the world. You can't rely on your favorite soap operas to keep you informed about the current trends in business. So put down your munchies and flavored coffee and make a concerted effort to stay "in the know" by subscribing to print magazines and online newsletters

3) FLEXIBILITY

When I think about flexibility, the childhood rhyme "Jack be nimble, Jack be quick, Jack jump over the candlestick" comes to mind. In order to keep from being burned, small businesses need to be nimble and quick. This means having the flexibility to act quickly in response to changes in the marketplace. Like a surfer riding a wave, you have to be in just the right place at the right time to ride the crest of the wave and get the best ride. Likewise, if small businesses monitor closely what's going on in the marketplace, they can act quickly to take advantage of current events and trends in the marketplace.

They say what gets measured, gets managed. Keep a close

eye on your monthly financials. Listen to your customers. Measure the effectiveness of your advertising. Then when you see a difference ask yourself, "was that good or bad" and ACT!

4) TAP INTO THE FIRE AND LET IT FUEL YOU

Simply said, small business owners want it more. Because of this, they will try harder and go the extra mile. That's why big companies like Wal-Mart and Saturn have made their employees part owners in the company. They have seen that people will work harder for themselves than for anyone else.

The best secret to success as an entrepreneur is to find something you are passionate about and create a business around that. When you do something you love you'll never "work" a day in your life. Entrepreneurs have that fire in their belly. Find a way to tap into that internal fire and let it fuel you to success.

5) VALUE

While big companies will often be able to offer the lower prices, small businesses will always be able to pile on the value. By offering better service, adding bonuses, giving and discounts on related products, the entrepreneurs can add more bang for the buck.

6) CREATIVE SPARK

"Exposing the Secrets of the 1%"

What's great about the entrepreneurs is that they aren't afraid to try something new. When I think of "creative spark", I think of my son, when he was three years old, eyeing a package of cookies up on top of the refrigerator. He doesn't know that it is up really high and that climbing up there is dangerous. He only sees the cookies and starts stacking chairs and climbing until I find him sitting on top of the fridge with a big smile and a mushy cookie face. Similarly, entrepreneurs don't "know" if something will work or not and fearlessly forge forward with their eyes on the prize. This innovation helps them to tap into new products, techniques, and processes.

They say, when the going gets tough, the tough gets going. When the market starts putting the heat on your business, ask yourself, are you staying "sharp"? Do you still have the entrepreneurial edge? By thinking like a start up, you will find that you will have the staying power to compete with the big boys on the block. And you'll find that kind of hard-earned success is "oh" so sweet!

Think Like an Entrepreneur

My biggest problem in becoming self-employed was me.

In order to BE a self-employed person I had to start thinking like one. I found myself reverting to that nine-to-five mentality. If I wasn't accomplishing a task every hour, then I must not really be working.

Sometimes a self-employed person has to make decisions about her business. Sometimes she is just thinking about a solution to a problem. Sometimes she just has to quiet her mind so new ideas can come. Just because you're not pounding away at the typewriter every minute doesn't mean you're not working.

I've also learned that it's okay NOT to answer the phone every time it rings. That's what voicemail is for, and the same goes for email. At my nine-to-five job I would leave the email program open all day and answer each one as it arrived. It took me a while to realize it's okay to only check email several times a day instead of constantly being interrupted. It's actually more productive than having to stop your thought process every time "you have mail." At my other job, I was able to let a phone call roll over into voice mail, but it took me a while to be able to shut down the email too.

You're going to have days where you feel you didn't accomplish much. Then again, you'll have days where you'll feel you can conquer the world and you'll be amazed at how much you got done. Some days you may not finish many tasks, but you'll make a decision on a problem that needed to be addressed. Or, you will have learned a valuable lesson about yourself.

And, I had to learn to stop breaking down all my tasks into dollars and cents. I tended to worry about how much I was or was not earning every day. The truth is, some days you're going to make more than other days. If I spent my day on marketing issues, even though I didn't earn any money from it that day, I would benefit from it sometime in the future.

Rather than worry about what benefits I do or don't have, I realized the benefit I have in my business is that I answer only to me. Everything I do will benefit me sooner or later. Instead of my income being dependent on somebody else's budget, I can go as far as I dream.

And because I'm now doing what I truly love and not what someone else tells me to, I'm much happier and more content. I learned if you start THINKING like an entrepreneur, then you'll actually be one.

"Exposing the Secrets of the 1%"

DISCLAMER:

The opinions expressed represent my own and not those of any artists, entrepreneurs, or individuals mentioned.

All the information and photos provided are for educational and inspirational use only. The Author makes no representation as to the accuracy, completeness, correctness, suitability, or validity of any information written and will not be liable for any errors, omissions, or delays in information or any losses, injuries, or damages arising from its display or use.

www.ingramcontent.com/pod-product-compliance
Lightning Source LLC
Chambersburg PA
CBHW051335170526
45166CB00002B/822